3.95
5J
6/07
QN

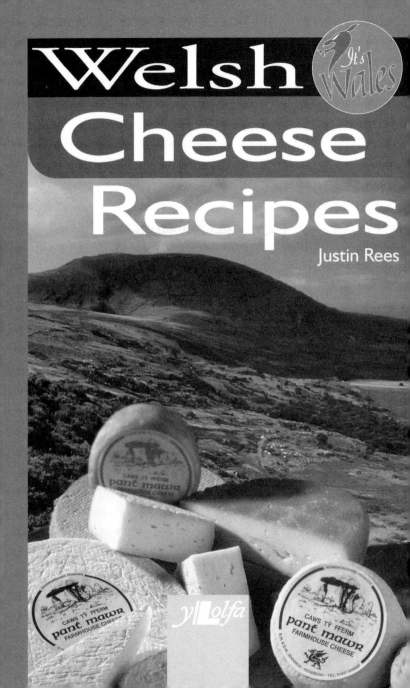

Welsh

It's Wales

Cheese

Recipes

Justin Rees

y Lolfa

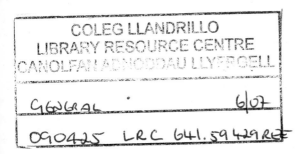
Photographs courtesy of Pant Mawr Farmhouse Cheeses, Caws Llanboidy, Caws Celtica, Caws Ffermdy Nantybwla, and Caws Cenarth

Cover design: Ceri Jones

ISBN: 0 86243 721 0

Printed on acid-free and partly recycled paper
and published and bound in Wales by
Y Lolfa Cyf., Talybont, Ceredigion SY24 5AP
e-mail ylolfa@ylolfa.com
website www.ylolfa.com
tel (01970) 832 304
fax 832 782

Contents

Introduction

In the past, farmhouse butter and cheese were made on every smallholding throughout Wales, and the old barrel butter churn was part of every kitchen.

Milk provided a stable income for many farms until quotas changed the perspective. Innovative families turned this to their advantage, and began producing value-added products such as butter, yoghurt and cheese – once again rekindling arts that were almost forgotten.

Now, along the valleys of the Towy, Cleddau, Teifi and Dee you can find skilled individuals producing farmhouse dairy products.

The range of cheeses varies from soft to hard, creamy to fully mature, and from hard Cheddar to Caerphilly. Also, many other washed-rind semi-soft and continental styles were developed by the University College of Wales, Aberystwyth early in the 20th century, and these are still used today.

Tips on Storing Cheese

Cheese should not be stored in conditions that are too cold. The best place to keep cheese is in a cool cellar, but not all of us are lucky enough to have one, so if you are like me, keep it in the refrigerator.

Protect the cheese by placing it in a plastic bag in an airtight container. Place it in the least cold part of the refrigerator, at the bottom or in one of the compartments in the door. Never freeze cheese, and do not wrap different cheeses together – every cheese has its own distinctive flavour and, if wrapped together, their flavours will mingle.

Always allow cheese to reach room temperature before eating. The time it takes to reach room temperature depends on the type of cheese, and how cold it has been stored.

Always remember never to overcook cheese, or it will become tough and stringy.

The Cheeses

Aeron Valley

Aeron Valley Cheese make quality Welsh Cheddar Cheese with locally-sourced milk from the lush pastures of the Aeron Valley. Farmhouse and Vintage Cheddars are their specialities.

Recipes: *Baked Mussels*
               Baked Apple with Pineapple and Welsh Cheddar
               Welsh Moussaka
               Welsh Cheddar Savoury Cheese Muffins
               Poppy Seed Cheese Loaf

Caerfai

Caerfai is a Cheddar-style cheese with leeks and garlic from Haverfordwest.

Recipe: *Aubergine Towers with Flat Mushrooms
              and Caerfai*

Caernarfon

South Caernarfon Creameries was established in 1938. The creamery is in one of the most picturesque areas of north west Wales, the Llŷn Peninsula in the foothills of Snowdonia, which is famous for its breathtaking scenery and natural beauty. It initially had 63 producer members, from whom churns of milk were collected daily. It now has its own fleet of road tankers that can be seen across Wales, and the company is universally renowned for its award-winning cheeses, which are made mainly from Friesian cows' milk.

Recipe: *Corn and Caernarfon Cheese Salad*

Caerphilly

The most famous of Welsh cheeses, Caerphilly is a fresh, white, mild cheese with a delicate, slightly salted and lightly acidic flavour. With a moderately firm, creamy and open texture it was originally made a century and a half ago and eaten by hard-working Welsh miners. Apparently, the cheese's saltiness replenished the salt lost from their bodies when mining. These days, Caerphilly's distinctive flavour is enjoyed more above ground with a Zinfandel or a white Lambrusco. The process for making Caerphilly is long and complicated – after curdling at 89° the curd is cut into cubes, stirred and dumped into cheese cloths, but the delicious end-product is worth the wait.

In 1987, Caws Cenarth Cheese revived the manufacture of traditional Welsh farmhouse Caerphilly cheesemaking, and is the longest-established Welsh Farmhouse Caerphilly cheesemaker in Wales. Caws Cenarth and Teifi Cheese (see under 'Teifi') produce an oak-smoked Caerphilly.

Recipes: *Caerphilly Cheese and Strawberry-filled Melon*
             Chicken and Smoked Caerphilly Cheese Wraps
             Cheesy Bacon Mashed Potato with Leeks
             Rack of Lamb with Welsh Rarebit
             Justin's Welsh Ploughman's
             Skate with a Trio of Welsh Cheeses
             Caerphilly Cheese Dip with a Mexican Bite
             Apple Pie with Caerphilly Pastry

Caws Celtica

Caws Celtica are farmhouse cheeses made from the unpasteurised milk of pedigree Friesland milking sheep at Capel Gwnda Farm, Rhydlewis, in west Wales. The sheep are all grazed on chemical-free south-facing hills above the valley of the River Ceri in the clean, unpolluted, rural landscape of Ceredigion, just a few miles from the coastline of Cardigan Bay. They are watered from an ancient holy healing well located on the farm, once renowned for its healing cures. The Lammas and Beltane cheeses are all hand-crafted using traditional farmhouse recipes.

Recipes: *Lammas Cheese and Nut Croquettes*
               Walnut Cheese Balls

Celtic Promise

Celtic Promise is the only Welsh cheese to have clinched the prestigious title of Supreme Champion at the British Cheese Awards. It has a rich creamy texture. Celtic Promise begins life as Teifi cheese (see under 'Teifi'). It is then ripened in cider by a Sussex cheesemaker, giving it the distinctive orange rind and fruity smell.

Recipe: *Grilled Chicory and Celtic Promise*
               with Carmarthen Ham

Green Thunder

The Snowdonia Cheese Company offer distinctively-flavoured cheese produced by a group of 80 traditional family farmers that are an integral part of the beautiful north Wales landscape. Intriguing flavours are available, such as Green Thunder, a mature Cheddar with garlic and garden herbs;

Red Devil, a Red Leicester with chilli and crushed red pepper; Purple Passion, a mild Cheddar with chocolate chips; and Ginger Spice, a medium-mature Cheddar with stem ginger.

Recipe: *Snowdonia Fruity Ham French Bread Pizza*

Harlech
Harlech is a mature smooth-textured Cheddar which blends the intense flavour of horseradish with parsley, coated in a distinctive bright orange wax.

Recipes: *Cheese on Toast with Ale*
            Justin's Welsh Ploughman's

Lancych
A matured, firm cow's milk cheese from Caws Cenarth.

Recipe: *Lancych, Watercress and Orange Baked*
            Pitta Bread Pockets

Llanboidy
Traditional Llanboidy Cheeses have been produced on the Cilowen Farm in west Wales since 1985. They are are made with the unpasteurised milk of a pedigree herd of the rare breed Red Poll cattle, which originated from a cross between the old Suffolk and Norfolk cattle of the 19th Century. The unique qualities of this old breed of cows' milk, combined with the traditional pastures they graze and the waters they drink from the farm's own well, are essential ingredients for the production of the natural and wholesome milk that is the key to the cheese that has been called the "Natural Taste of Wales". This cheese has an exceptionally smooth, almost silky,

texture that contrasts with its robust flavour. It is a hard pressed cheese and, as with all farmhouse cheeses, its taste varies with maturity and season. Llanboidy with Laverbread Cheese is made with the famous edible seaweed harvested from the south west Wales coastline, giving the cheese an attractive speckled appearance. The cheeses have won the Gold Medal and the Best Organic Cheese award at the British Cheese Awards.

Recipes: *Llanboidy with Laverbread Fritters*
             Llanboidy with Cockles
             Justin's Welsh Ploughman's
             Skate with a Trio of Welsh Cheeses

Llandyrnog

Llandyrnog Creamery in Denbighshire has been established for over 80 years. Situated in the heart of the Welsh countryside, it produces a range of prize-winning Cheddars.

Recipes: *Lobster in a Crisp Champagne Batter with a*
             Llandyrnog Cheese Sauce
             Welsh Cheddar Cheese Soup

Llangloffan

Llangloffan is a hard-pressed Cheshire-type of Cheddar, made since the late 1970s in Llangloffan, between Fishguard and Haverfordwest in Pembrokeshire. Red Llangloffan contains herbs and garlic.

Recipes: *Cinnamon Llangloffan Toasts*
             Red Llangloffan Rosti
             Skate with a Trio of Welsh Cheeses
             Cauliflower and Llangloffan Cheese Salad

Merlin

This is a hard goat's cheese made by Merlin Cheeses in mid Wales. Made from unpasteurised Welsh goat's milk, the cheese is coated in wax and comes in an astounding variety of delicious flavours such as Smoked, Garlic and Chives, Herbs, Celery, Apple, Pineapple, Peaches, Ginger, Pear and Cinnamon, Walnut, and Olives.

Recipe: *Merlin Mild Goat's Cheese Bruschetta*

Nantybwla

Nantybwla Farmhouse Cheese is a Caerphilly-type cheese, hand-made in Carmarthen since 1985. It is from an old traditional family recipe, using Holstein and Jersey cows' milk.

Recipes: *Glamorgan Cherry Tomato Kebabs*
           Skate with a Trio of Welsh Cheeses

Nantybwla Curd Cheese is a young cheese taken off halfway through the process of making Nantybwla Caerphilly, which is a semi-soft cheese with a delicate taste.

Recipe: *Carmarthen Seafood Salad*

Old Shire

Old Shire is a traditionally-made mature cheese made by South Caernarfon Creameries (see 'Caernarfon'). Its distinctive flavour and texture are characteristic of traditionally-made cheese.

Recipes: *Smoked Salmon Cheese Parcels*
           Welsh Cheddar Cheese Soup
           Caernarfon Cheese Pudding
           Old Shire Italian-style Stuffed Peppers

Pant Mawr

Pant Mawr Farmhouse Cheeses in Rosebush, Pembrokeshire have been producing cheese for 15 years. You can buy Pant Mawr Farm goat's milk curd cheese packaged in plain olive oil, chilli oil, or garlic oil.

Recipes: *Pant Mawr Beetroot Dip*
                Pant Mawr Baked Cheesecake

Pantysgawn

Pantysgawn Goat's Cheese is a natural mild soft cheese, with a creamy taste and light texture.

Recipes: *Leek and Pantysgawn Goat's Cheese Parcels*
                Stuffed Trout with Pantysgawn Goat's Cheese
                Pantysgawn Coconut Cannelloni with
                Raspberry Sauce

Perl Las and Perl Wen

These cheeses are made by Caws Cenarth Cheese. Mould ripened, Perl Wen is a new style of semi-soft creamy cheese combining the freshness of a Caerphilly with the outer rind of a Brie. In 2000, Perl Wen received a Silver Award for the Best New Cheese at the World Cheese Awards and a first at the Royal Welsh Show 2002. Perl Las was joint winner in the Organic food awards 2002 cheese category out of 90 cheeses from all over the world. The judges at the Organic Food Awards described Perl Las as 'original and unique; lovely and strong; creamy with an intense lingering aftertaste'.

Recipe: *Perl Wen Chicken and Spinach Pies*
              Welsh Black Fillet Steak with Port Wine
              and Perl Las Melt

Smoked Cerwyn

Smoked Cerwyn is produced by Pant Mawr (see 'Pant Mawr'). This is a creamy textured cheese which is smoked young to provide moist flesh. Affectionately named after the highest mountain in the Preseli range, this young cows' milk cheese has a mellow flavour. A tender hard cheese, it matures naturally for a short period, resulting in a distinctively mild cheese. It was the Silver Award Winner at the British Cheese Awards 2003, and the Gold Award Winner at the World Cheese Awards 2001.

Recipes: Grilled Sardines with Apple and Smoked Cerwyn Cheese Stuffing
Smoked Goat's Cheese Drumsticks

St Illtyd

St Illtyd is a mature cheddar with white wine, garlic and herbs, with a black wax cover.

Recipe: Cheese and Chilli Con Carne Tart

Teifi

Teifi Farmhouse Cheese was established in 1982. A Gouda-style cheese, Teifi is buttery, dense and smooth with a light sweetness when young; the longer it is matured, the more it develops its sweet, toffee-like flavour. Smaller cheeses flavoured with garlic, garlic and onion, celery, nettle (a traditional Dutch flavouring), sweet pepper, chives, seaweed, mustard seed and cumin seed are also made. Caerphilly is produced as well, using unpasteurised Frieisian milk from the neighbouring farm, and utilising the traditional method of cutting the curds by hand, resulting in a crumblier, moister cheese, that can be matured on.

Recipes: *Pork Sausage and Teifi Cheese Potato Pie*
         Chicken and Smoked Caerphilly Cheese Wraps

Tintern

Tintern Cheddar Cheese takes its name from Tintern Abbey, which was founded by Cistercian monks. It is a Welsh mature Cheddar with fresh chives and shallots giving a creamy texture.

Recipes: *Tintern Cheese Spread*
         Tintern Kiwi Salad

Y Fenni

A Welsh cheese with wholegrain mustard seed and Welsh ale, it is coated in a cream-coloured wax, and it has a full tangy mustard flavour, moist texture, and a pale-yellow colouring speckled with the mustard grains. Y Fenni is often enjoyed as part of a ploughman's lunch. Its consistency makes it excellent when melted, and it can be served on toast or even on a steak.

Recipe: *Pumpkin and Cheese Soup*

Starters, Salads, Side Dishes and Snacks

Llanboidy with Laverbread Fritters

Serves 2

170g/6½ oz Llanboidy Cheese with Laverbread, cut into strips
½–¾ cup milk
2 tbsp butter, melted
1 egg, separated
90g/3½ oz flour
pinch salt
vinegar
oil or butter for frying

Beat together milk, melted butter and egg yolk, mix with flour and salt until a smooth consistency.

Fold in stiffly beaten egg white.

Dip strips of Llanboidy Cheese in vinegar, then in batter mixture and fry on both sides in hot oil or butter until golden brown on both sides.

Llanboidy with Cockles

Serves 4

75g/3 oz Llanboidy Cheese
50g/2 oz laverbread
75g/3 oz bacon, chopped
75g/3 oz cockles
½ cup of cream

Fry bacon in pan, then add cockles and laverbread. Stir well.

Add cream. Simmer until sauce starts to thicken.

Place in ovenproof dish, then put slices of Llanboidy Cheese on the top.

Place under the grill or in the oven until cheese has melted and turned a golden brown.

Merlin Mild Goat's Cheese Bruschetta

Serves 2

1 small baguette or ciabatta loaf
2 tbsp olive oil
1 garlic clove
100g/4 oz Merlin Goat's Cheese
2 spring onions, chopped
1 tbsp parsley, chopped

Mash the Merlin Goat's Cheese with the spring onions and parsley. Season with salt and pepper.

Slice the baguette and brush each slice with olive oil and garlic clove.

Spoon over the cheese mixture and grill until the cheese melts.

Smoked Salmon Cheese Parcels

Serves 2

100g/4 oz ready sliced smoked salmon
150g/6 oz Old Shire Cheese
2 leaves lollo rosso lettuce
4 lemon wedges
1 tbsp salad dressing

Cut Old Shire Cheese into small batons about 1cm by 2cm.

Wrap slices of smoked salmon around cheese, garnish with lollo rosso lettuce and lemon wedges.

Drizzle with salad dressing to serve.

Cheese on Toast with Ale

Serves 4

225g/8 oz Harlech Cheese, grated
50g/2 oz butter
4 tbsp brown ale
1 tbsp mustard powder
salt and cracked black pepper
cayenne pepper
4 thick slices of bread

Melt the butter in a pan, then add mustard and brown ale, grated Harlech Cheese and seasoning.

Stir well until mixture looks creamy and the cheese has almost melted. Take care not to boil. Remove mixture from heat.

Toast both sides of the bread, then evenly place cheese mixture onto toast and place under grill until hot and bubbling.

To serve, sprinkle with cayenne pepper.

Lammas Cheese and Nut Croquettes

Serves 3–4

75g/3 oz Lammas Cheese, grated
1 cup nuts, finely chopped
2 cups fresh breadcrumbs
1 small onion
1 tbsp parsley, chopped
pinch nutmeg
salt and pepper
1 egg, beaten
milk

Place all ingredients except milk in a bowl and mix well.

Stir in just enough milk to make a stiff paste.

Roll into croquettes.

Place on a greased oven tray and bake for 20 minutes at 180°C/ 350°F/Gas mark 4.

Walnut Cheese Balls

Serves 6

225g/8 oz Beltane Ewe's Cheese
60g/2 oz mayonnaise
3–4 cherries, chopped
mint, chopped
salt and pepper
60g/2 oz walnuts, chopped

Mix together Beltane Ewe's Cheese, mayonnaise and fresh or glacé cherries.

Season to taste with chopped mint, salt and pepper.

Mould into balls and roll in chopped walnuts.

Tintern Cheese Spread

225g/8 oz Tintern Cheddar, grated
115g/4 oz butter
2 eggs, beaten
½ tsp salt
1 tsp mustard

Combine all the ingredients and mix well.

Place in a saucepan, slowly bring to the boil and simmer for 2 minutes.

Leave to cool and store in the refrigerator.

Tintern Kiwi Salad

Serves 3–4

1 small lettuce, shredded
2 oranges, segmented
3 kiwi fruit, sliced
115g/4 oz cashew nuts
115g/4 oz Tintern Cheddar, cubed

Dressing
2 tbsp vegetable oil
1 tbsp cider vinegar or malt vinegar
½ tsp salt
¼ tsp cayenne pepper

Mix all dressing ingredients together in a screw-top jar and shake well.

Toss shredded lettuce in half the dressing mixture, and spread on a flat dish.

Arrange orange and kiwi around the dish in layers.

Finish with nuts and Tintern Cheddar in the centre.
Pour over remaining dressing.

Goes well with game.

Cauliflower and Llangloffan Cheese Salad

Serves 4

½ small cauliflower, broken into florets
½ cup radishes, sliced
I small onion, finely diced
oil and vinegar dressing
60g/2 oz Llangloffan Cheese

Reserve several radishes for decorating.

Combine cauliflower with remaining radishes and onion.

Toss with dressing.

Crumble in Llangloffan Cheese and toss again lightly.

Corn and Caernarfon Cheese Salad

Serves 4

285g/10 oz whole-kernel corn
115g/4 oz Caernarfon Cheddar Cheese, cubed
¼ medium cabbage, shredded
3 shallots, finely diced

Dressing
¼ cup mayonnaise
¼ cup sour cream
1 tbsp white vinegar
salt and pepper

Place corn, cheese, cabbage and shallots in a bowl and toss with a mixture of mayonnaise, sour cream and vinegar just before serving. Season to taste with salt and pepper.

Lancych, Watercress and Orange Baked Pitta Bread Pockets

Serves 4

4 pitta bread
350g/12 oz Lancych Cheese, sliced
handful of watercress
2 oranges, segmented
1 can of anchovy fillets, drained

Make a slit down one side of pitta bread so it forms a pocket.

Fill with the ingredients and bake in the oven for 5 minutes at 180°C/350°F/Gas mark 4.

Grilled Chicory and Celtic Promise with Carmarthen Ham

Serves 4

200g/7 oz Carmarthen Ham
4 heads chicory
2 medium heads radicchio
2 tbsp walnut oil
150g/3oz Celtic Promise Cheese, grated
1 tbsp rosemary
45ml/2 fl oz fromage frais
rind of 1 orange, finely grated

Cut the heads of chicory lengthways in half.

Cut each radicchio into 8 wedges.

Pre-heat grill.

Lay out the chicory and radicchio on baking tray and brush with walnut oil.

Grill for 2–3 minutes.

Sprinkle over grated Celtic Promise, then scatter fromage frais, rosemary and orange shreds with strips of Carmarthen Ham over the warm chicory and radicchio heads.

Carmarthen Ham

Cured in the traditional Welsh farmhouse way under controlled temperature conditions, Carmarthen Ham is then dried to mature. Sliced thinly and pre-packed for convenience, it can be served in many ways.

Snowdonia Fruity Ham French Bread Pizza

Serves 4

2 small baguettes
½ pint tomato sauce
75g/3 oz ham or bacon
4 pineapple rings, chopped
½ small green pepper, sliced
50g/2 oz Green Thunder Mature Cheddar with Garlic and Herbs, grated
salt and pepper

Preheat oven to 200°C/400°F/Gas mark 6.

Cut baguettes in half lengthways and toast until golden brown. Spread tomato sauce over baguette.

Slice ham and lay on baguette with chopped pineapple and sliced peppers.

Sprinkle Green Thunder Mature Cheddar on top and bake for about 15 minutes until crisp and golden.

Cinnamon Llangloffan Toasts

Serves 2

25g/1oz unsalted butter
large pinch of ground cinnamon
2 slices of raisin bread, cut in half and toasted
1 ripe pear, peeled, cored and sliced
1 tbsp lemon juice
75g/3oz Llangloffan Cheese, crumbled
ground cinnamon and brown sugar to decorate

Preheat grill.

Beat together the butter and cinnamon until well mixed, and spread on the toasted bread. Brush the pear slices with lemon juice and arrange on the toast with the slices overlapping each other. Sprinkle over the Llangloffan Cheese, then grill the toast until the cheese starts bubbling and turns golden brown.

Sprinkle with sugar and cinnamon and serve immediately.

Red Llangloffan Rosti

Serves 4

350g/12 oz potatoes, unpeeled
3 tbsp sunflower oil
1 small onion, chopped
3 rashers of streaky bacon, chopped
100g/4 oz Red Llangloffan, cubed
seasoning
chopped fresh dill to garnish

Boil the potatoes for 6 minutes until nearly tender.

Drain, cool for 5 minutes, then remove the skin and grate coarsely.

Heat 1 tbsp of oil in a small frying pan and cook the onion and bacon for 5 minutes until lightly brown.

Add the bacon mixture and the Red Llangloffan to the potato, mix together and season.

Clean the pan then heat the remaining oil.

Add the potato mixture and quickly pat into a cake, then cook over a medium heat until lightly brown.

Carefully tip out onto a plate and slide back into the pan uncooked side down; cook until golden.

Turn the rosti onto a serving plate and sprinkle with dill.

Caerphilly Cheese and Strawberry Filled Melon

Serves 4

2 small Ogen or Charentais melons
100g/4 oz Caerphilly Cheese, cubed
5cm cucumber, diced
100g/4 oz wild strawberries, quartered

Dressing
1 tbsp vinegar
3 tbsp olive oil
½ tsp mustard powder
salt and ground black pepper to taste
1 tsp sugar

Cut the melons in half and scoop out the seeds; set the halves aside.

Mix together the Caerphilly Cheese, cucumber and strawberries.

Mix all dressing ingredients together in a screw-top jar and shake well.

Put mixture into the melon halves and pour over the dressing mixture.

Chicken and Smoked Caerphilly Cheese Wraps

Serves 4

2 cooked chicken breasts, thinly sliced
½ small iceberg lettuce, finely chopped
4 spring onions, finely chopped
1 carrot, grated
1 beef tomato, finely diced
¼ raddichio lettuce, finely shredded
175g/6 oz Teifi Oak-smoked Caerphilly Cheese, grated
4 tbsp mayonnaise
salt and pepper to season
4 tortilla pancakes

Mix all ingredients together in a large bowl then divide mix between 4 tortilla pancakes.

Place in the centre of the pancake and fold both sides together, then roll the opposite ends to form a spring roll-type shape.

Slice tortilla rolls in half at an angle, and serve.

Great as a snack or for buffets.

Cheesy Bacon Mashed Potato with Leeks

Serves 3–4

700g/1lb 7 oz old potatoes
15g/½ oz butter
splash of milk
2 bacon rashers, cooked and finely diced
25g/1 oz Caerphilly Cheese
1 small leek, finely chopped

Peel potatoes and cut into walnut-sized cubes.

Place into a pan of salted water, bring to the boil, cook for about 15 minutes until soft, then add chopped leeks.

Drain out all but a little splash of water from the pan and mash, together with butter, Caerphilly Cheese, and a little milk.

Sprinkle on the chopped bacon and serve.

Main Courses – Vegetarian, Meat and Fish

Glamorgan Cherry Tomato Kebabs

Serves 6

4 tbsp vegetable oil
I small garlic clove, chopped
I leek, finely chopped
150g/6 oz Nantybwla Farmhouse Cheese, grated
2 tbsp parsley, chopped
½ tsp dry mustard powder
150g/6 oz fresh breadcrumbs
I egg, beaten
24 cherry tomatoes
seasoning

Pan fry leek and garlic in 1 tbsp of oil for a couple of minutes until soft.

Mix in grated Nantybwla Cheese, parsley, mustard and breadcrumbs.

Add the egg, then stir in to bind the mixture together.

Season and leave to stand in fridge for 30 minutes.

Shape cheese mixture into small balls; thread the balls onto skewers, alternating with cherry tomatoes.

Heat remaining oil in large pan.

Cook the kebabs, turning gently and letting them brown evenly without burning or breaking.

Baked Apple with Pineapple and Welsh Cheddar

Serves 2

1 small apple, sliced in half
1 pineapple, finely chopped
50g/2 oz Aeron Valley Cheddar, grated
1 tsp parsley, chopped
cinnamon to taste

Scoop out the core and pips of the apple with a teaspoon, and discard.

Mix together chopped pineapple, Aeron Valley Cheddar and parsley.

Place in the apple halves and bake in the oven at 180°C/350°F/Gas mark 4 for approximately 10 minutes until the cheese has melted and is golden in colour.

Makes a great vegetarian starter, savoury dessert, or garnish for pork or chicken.

Aubergine Towers with Flat Mushrooms and Caerfai

Serves 4

Tomato Sauce
2 tbsp olive oil
I large onion, thinly sliced
2–3 cloves garlic
440g/1lb can plum tomatoes, roughly chopped
I tsp dried basil
I cup red wine
2 tsp sugar
salt and cracked black pepper

Mushrooms
8 flat mushrooms
2 tbsp olive oil
salt and pepper

Aubergines
I aubergine
salt and pepper
2 tbsp olive oil
400g/14 oz Caerfai Cheese

Sauce – heat oil in a heavy-based pan and cook the onions and garlic until soft.

Stir in tomatoes and their juices, then add basil and red wine.

Cover and simmer for about 40 minutes.

Add sugar and season to taste.

Simmer for a further 10 minutes. Set aside and keep warm.

Mushrooms – brush mushrooms with oil and season.

Pan fry or grill whole. Set aside and keep warm.

Aubergines – cut aubergine into 1cm thick discs and season.

Pan fry in the olive oil until browned on both sides.

Slice Caerfai Cheese and place on top of each aubergine disc.

Grill until cheese melts.

To serve – divide tomato sauce onto four plates.

Place one aubergine disc on top of each serving of sauce, and top in turn with mushrooms. Repeat until all ingredients are used, making four stacks.

Rack of Lamb with Welsh Rarebit

Serves 4

4 250g/9 oz lamb racks, trimmed
50g/2 oz butter
50g/2 oz flour
150ml/5 fl oz milk
100ml/3½ fl oz double cream
1 tsp mustard
Worcester sauce
2 eggs, well beaten
100g/4 oz Caerphilly Cheese, grated
sprig of rosemary and thyme
salt and pepper

Three-quarter roast lamb racks in oven with rosemary and thyme.

Melt the butter in a saucepan. Blend in the flour and cook for a minute.

Then add the milk and cream, slowly stirring constantly.

Once the mixture starts to bubble, take off the heat and add the mustard and Worcester sauce. Beat the eggs, then stir them into sauce, and fold in grated Caerphilly Cheese.

Spoon mixture over the lamb racks and return to the oven until golden brown.

Old Shire Italian-Style Stuffed Peppers

Serves 4

2 large peppers
400g/14 oz fresh ripe tomatoes, finely chopped
50g/2 oz mushrooms, finely sliced
40g/1½ oz capers, finely chopped
10 anchovy fillets, finely chopped
2 garlic cloves, finely chopped
4 tbsp parsley, chopped
75g/3 oz fresh breadcrumbs
50g/2 oz Old Shire Cheese
2 tsp Worcestershire Sauce
½ tsp ground nutmeg
5 tbsp olive oil
salt and pepper to season

Preheat the oven to 200°C/400°F/Gas mark 6.

Slice each pepper in half lengthways, and remove the stalk and seeds.

Mix together the tomatoes, mushrooms, capers, anchovies, garlic, parsley, breadcrumbs, Old Shire Cheese, Worcestershire Sauce and nutmeg. Fill the peppers with the mixture.

Grease a large ovenproof dish with 2 tbsp olive oil.

Arrange peppers in dish; pour the remaining oil over peppers and season.

Smoked Goat's Cheese Drumsticks

Serves 3

6 chicken drumsticks
75g/3oz Smoked Cerwyn Goat's Cheese
6 rashers streaky bacon
oil or melted butter for cooking
salt and pepper
8 wooden cocktail sticks

Pre-heat oven at 180°C/350°F/Gas mark 4, make a deep incision in the thickest part of each drumstick and pack the deep slit with Smoked Goat's Cheese.

Season with salt and pepper, then wrap streaky bacon tightly around each drumstick, ensuring the slits are covered, then secure with a cocktail stick.

Smear each drumstick with a little butter or oil.

Cook in the oven for 15–20 minutes.

Pork Sausage and Teifi Cheese Potato Pie

Serves 6

900g/2lb floury potatoes
450g/1lb pork sausages
2 tbsp parsley, chopped
50g/2 oz butter
275ml/½ pint milk
¼ tsp nutmeg
100g/4 oz Teifi Cheese, grated
2 egg yolks, beaten
salt and pepper
butter for greasing

Wash and peel potatoes and cook in boiling salted water until soft.

Skin the sausages and crumble with a fork.

Fry them in their own fat until the meat is brown.

Pre-heat oven to 180°C/350°F/Gas mark 4.

Mash potatoes, add parsley and butter, and beat well. Add enough milk to cover the potatoes, and a sprinkle of nutmeg.

Then add the grated Teifi Cheese, egg yolks, sausage meat and salt and pepper, beating well.

Place in a well-buttered baking dish and bake in the oven for 20–30 minutes or until the top is a golden brown.

Cheese and Chilli Con Carne Tart

Serves 4

2 cups self-raising flour
25g/1 oz butter
¾ cup St Illtyd Cheddar Cheese, grated
2 tbsp fresh thyme or parsley
¾ cup milk
425g/15 oz tinned chilli con carne
1 courgette, trimmed and grated
milk to glaze
½ cup St Illtyd Cheddar Cheese, grated, for topping

Sift the flour into a bowl, and rub in the butter until the mixture resembles fine crumbs.

Stir in the St Illtyd Cheddar and thyme or parsley.

Stir in the milk to form a soft dough, and knead lightly until smooth.

Roll the dough out on a floured board to about a 30cm diameter circle. Place the dough over the base and sides of a 24cm flan or cake tin, allowing the edges to overhang.

Combine the chilli corn carne and courgette and pile into the tin.

Flip the edges over and brush with milk to glaze.

Sprinkle the second measure of St Illtyd Cheddar over the top.

Bake at 200°C/400°F/Gas mark 6 for 20 minutes until golden brown.

Perl Wen Chicken and Spinach Pies

Serves 4

4 boneless chicken breasts, skinned
250g/9 oz frozen chopped spinach, defrosted
2 tbsp cream cheese
175g/6 oz chopped Perl Wen Cheese
¼ tsp nutmeg
¼ tsp salt
¼ tsp white pepper
2 sheets frozen pre-rolled puff pastry, defrosted
milk to glaze

Remove skin from chicken breast.

Squeeze the spinach between two plates to remove all excess moisture – the spinach needs to be really dry, or you may end up with soggy pastry when the pies cook.

Mix the spinach, cream cheese, Perl Wen Cheese, nutmeg, salt and pepper.

Take the pastry sheets and cut in half diagonally.

Place a quarter of the spinach mixture in the centre of each triangle, and place a chicken breast on the top. Bring the ends down to cover the chicken, and fold the thicker corner on top, to completely enclose.

Pinch ends together, then transfer to a greased tray. Brush with milk to glaze.

Bake at 220°C/425°F/Gas mark 7 for 15–20 minutes until golden.

Welsh Black Fillet Steak
with Port Wine and Perl Las Melt

Serves 4

4 225g/8 oz Welsh Black fillet steaks
200g/7 oz Perl Las Cheese
25g/1 oz cooking oil
25g/1 oz butter

Port Wine Sauce
250ml/9 fl oz ruby port
100g/4 oz demerara sugar

Heat the oil and the butter – an oil-and-butter mix prevents burning. Pan fry steaks to taste. Remove from pan and pour in port and demerara sugar. Reduce by half.

Slice Perl Las Cheese and place on top of steak. Grill until cheese has melted.

Serve on plate with port sauce around.

Welsh Moussaka

Serves 3–4

2 aubergines
4–6 tbsp oil
I large onion, chopped
I leek, chopped
2 garlic cloves
450g/Ilb minced Welsh lamb
425g/15 oz can of chopped tomatoes
2 tsp tomato puree
25g/I oz Aeron Valley Cheddar Cheese
25g/I oz butter
25g/I oz plain flour
300ml/½ pint milk
I egg, beaten
seasoning

Slice aubergine and place in a large colander. Sprinkle with salt, and set aside for 30 minutes to draw out the juices.

Heat 2 tbsp oil in a large pan and gently fry onions, leek and garlic for about 15 minutes.

Add the minced lamb and fry until brown.

Pre-heat oven to 200°C/400°F/Gas mark 6. Drain aubergines and rinse in cold water. Fry in remaining oil until golden, then drain on kitchen paper.

Arrange a layer of aubergine in an oven-proof dish, cover with half the mince, another layer of aubergine, then the remaining mince, and finish with a layer of aubergine.

Melt the butter in a pan. Stir in flour, then gradually stir in the milk. Bring to the boil, stirring until thick. Remove from heat and beat in the egg and Aeron Valley Cheddar.

Spoon the sauce over the aubergine and bake for 30 minutes until browned on top.

Justin's Welsh Ploughman's

Serves 1–2

**3 slices of various Welsh Cheeses of your choice
(preferably Harlech, Llanboidy with Laverbread, and
Caerphilly)**
1 slice of peppered roasted ham
1 whole apple
1 whole ripe tomato
2 large pickles
1 tbsp Branston pickle
1 small carrot, cut into batons
crusty bread
dollop of butter

Arrange on a plate, and enjoy!

Grilled Sardines with Apple and Smoked Cerwyn Cheese Stuffing

Serves 4

4 fresh sardines, cleaned
50g/2 oz butter
I apple, grated
4 spring onions, finely chopped
50g/2 oz Smoked Cerwyn Cheese
25g/I oz fresh breadcrumbs
zest of half an orange, grated
4 tbsp orange juice
salt and pepper
orange wedges and parsley to garnish
8 wooden cocktail sticks

Pre-heat barbeque.

Clean and gut sardines. Remove heads, trim tails, and make three cuts across each side of fish. Melt 25g/1 oz butter in a small saucepan, add onions and cook until soft.

Stir the apple, Smoked Cerwyn Cheese, breadcrumbs and orange zest into the saucepan and season. Cool slightly.

Stuff each fish with the mixture and secure the slits with cocktail sticks.

Melt remaining butter and stir in orange juice.

Place sardines directly on a well-oiled grill, or wrap in foil and cook on high heat for about 5–8 minutes on each side. Baste with orange butter while cooking.

Remove the cocktail sticks and serve with orange wedges and parsley.

Skate with a Trio of Welsh Cheeses

Serves 4

4 skate wings
I tbsp butter
4 tbsp flour
2 egg yolks
½ cup of cream or milk
salt and pepper
½ cup of wine
120g/5 oz Llanboidy, Red Llangloffan, Nantybwla
Caerphilly Cheese
parsley, chopped

Steam the skate wings for 8 minutes in a covered pan, with half a cup of water and a splash of white wine. Reserve stock.

Melt the butter in a pan. Stir in the flour and cook for 3 minutes.

Whisk together the egg yolks and cream, then add the roux along with the fish stock and ½ cup of white wine. Bring to the boil, stirring continuously. Season to taste.

Pour sauce over the skate wings.

Sprinkle with grated or crumbled cheese and grill until cheese melts. Garnish with chopped parsley.

Baked Mussels

Serves 3

Sauce
60g/2 oz butter
6 sprigs parsley, finely chopped
2 cloves garlic, crushed
salt and pepper
2 tbsp Aeron Valley Cheddar, grated

30 mussels in shell
¾ cup white wine

Combine the sauce ingredients and mix well.

Boil the mussels in wine. When opened, remove from the liquid. Strain liquid and reserve. Discard one half of each shell, then place mussels on a large oven tray. Spread each one with sauce, sprinkle with a little liquid, and place under grill to brown.

Lobster in a Crisp Champagne Batter with a Llandyrnog Cheese Sauce

Serves 2

2 small lobster tails, sliced
oil for frying

Champagne Batter
¾ cup plain flour
¼ cup champagne
¼ cup soda water

Cheese Sauce
½ pint milk
½ pint single cream
I tsp mustard
25g/Ioz plain flour
40g/I ½ oz butter
50g/2 oz Llandyrnog Mature Cheddar, grated
pinch of cayenne pepper
½ tsp lemon juice
salt and pepper

Batter – sift flour into bowl, whisk together with champagne and soda water.

Sauce – place all ingredients except cheese, cayenne pepper and lemon juice in a saucepan, and whisk over heat until smooth and thick. Then add the Llandyrnog Mature Cheddar while stirring, and cook gently for 5 minutes. Season with salt, pepper, cayenne and lemon juice.

Dip lobster slices into batter mixture. Lightly fry in oil for 3–4 minutes until batter is crisp and golden, turning while cooking. Remove from oil and place on kitchen paper towel to remove excess oil. Serve on a dish, drizzled with cheese sauce.

Nice as a starter, or serve as a main course with salad and new potatoes.

Carmarthen Seafood Salad

Serves 4–6

8 scallops with roes attached
180g/6 oz monkfish, cubed
120g/4 oz prawns, cooked
120g/4 oz mussels, cooked
lemon juice

Dressing
120g/4 oz Nantybwla Curd Cheese
1–2 tbsp milk
4½ tbsp natural yogurt
salt and pepper
juice of ½ lemon
1 tsp Dijon mustard
1 tsp chilli powder
pinch of cayenne pepper

Pan fry monkfish in white wine and butter for 3–4 minutes.

Add ½ cup of boiling water, cook for another 4–5 minutes until scallops and monkfish are cooked, then stir in remaining fish.

Cook on high heat for 2–3 minutes. Leave to cool in the liquid then drain well.

Blend the Nantybwla Curd Cheese, milk and yoghurt in a food processor or blender, then stir in remaining ingredients. Toss the seafood in the dressing and serve.

Leek and Pantysgawn Goat's Cheese Parcels

Serves 4

2 medium-sized leeks
100g/4 oz fresh Pantysgawn Goat's Cheese
50g/2 oz walnuts, chopped
25g/1 oz raisins soaked in sherry for 30 minutes

Dressing
3 tbsp walnut oil
1 tbsp white wine vinegar
1 tsp clear honey
seasoning

Mix all dressing ingredients together in a screw-top jar and shake well.

Discard the tough outer layers of the leek, and wash under cold water.

Plunge the leeks into a large pan of boiling hot water for about 8 minutes.

Drain, and run under the cold tap to retain the bright green colour, then carefully peel off the layers of the leek, tearing them as little as possible. Reserve the best 8 layers and finely chop the rest.

Mix together the chopped leeks, Pantysgawn Goat's Cheese, walnuts and raisins, and divide into four portions.

Wrap each portion in two leek layers to form a parcel.

Arrange on a serving dish and spoon the dressing over each parcel.

Stuffed Trout with Pantysgawn Goat's Cheese

Serves 4

4 good-sized trout (brown is best; if not, rainbow)
1 tbsp fresh chives, chopped
1 lemon
8 rashers of smoked streaky bacon
225g/8 oz Pantysgawn Goat's Cheese
seasoning

Pre-heat oven to 180°C/350°F/Gas Mark 4.

Clean, gut and bone trout.

Put chopped chives and Pantysgawn Goat's Cheese in the belly of the fish. Squeeze over lemon juice.

Wrap each fish in 2 rashers of bacon and lay them side by side in a baking dish.

Bake for 15–20 minutes until the bacon is crisp and the trout flesh is a flaky texture.

Soups and Dips

Pumpkin and Cheese Soup

Serves 4

2 cups pumpkin
½ cup lentils, washed
4 cups stock or water
salt and pepper
90g/3 oz Y Fenni Cheese, grated

Add pumpkin and lentils to stock or water.

Bring to the boil and simmer for 1 hour. Season to taste and press through a coarse sieve or colander, return purée to saucepan and re-boil.

Remove and stir in grated Y Fenni Cheese.

Do not re-boil.

Welsh Cheddar Cheese Soup

For this dish, you can use any Welsh Cheddar such as Llandyrnog (mature or mild) or Old Shire Mature Cheddar.

Serves 6

600ml/1 pint clear stock
120g/4 oz rice
1 onion, roughly chopped
600ml/ 1 pint milk
120g/4 oz Welsh Cheddar Cheese, grated
salt and pepper to taste

Boil rice and onion in stock until mushy, using a saucepan with a tightly fitting lid. The rice will absorb most of the stock.

Rub through a sieve or use a blender; return mixture to the saucepan and add the milk.

Bring almost to boiling point.

Add seasonings and Welsh Cheddar Cheese just before serving.

Caerphilly Cheese Dip
with a Mexican Bite

Serves 6

1 tbsp oil
2 spring onions
2 tsp ground cumin
1 tsp ground coriander
300g/10 oz tomato salsa
125g/4 oz cream cheese
¼ cup of cream
1 ½ cups Caerphilly Cheese, grated
1 tbsp cornflour
pepper

Heat the oil in a saucepan and cook the spring onions, cumin and coriander for 2–3 mins until quite soft and fragrant.

Add the tomato salsa and cream cheese. Stir until melted.

Add the cream, grated Caerphilly Cheese and cornflour, and allow to cook over a very low heat, stirring constantly until thick. Season with pepper.

Serve in a large bowl with vegetable crudités, crusty bread, potato wedges and taco chips.

Pant Mawr Beetroot Dip

Serves 6

225g/8 oz Pant Mawr Goat's Cheese in Plain Olive Oil
1 tbsp mayonnaise
150ml/¼ pint natural yoghurt or sour cream
2 small cooked beetroots, grated

Mash the Pant Mawr Goat's Cheese in a bowl.

Stir in the mayonnaise and yoghurt (or sour cream).

Just before serving, stir in the beetroot.

Desserts, Breads and Puddings

Pantysgawn Coconut Cannelloni with Raspberry Sauce

Serves 6

18 cannelloni pasta
oil for deep frying
250g/9 oz Pantysgawn Goat's Cheese
2 tbsp Malibu
¼ cup of icing sugar

Sauce
150g/6 oz frozen or fresh raspberries
1 tbsp caster sugar

Place frozen raspberries and caster sugar in a pan and bring to the boil. Remove and purée, then pass through a fine sieve. Leave to cool.

In a large pan of boiling water, cook pasta until just tender. Drain and pat dry with paper towel.

Deep fry pasta until brown, and leave to cool.

Combine the Pantysgawn Goat's Cheese, coconut, Malibu and icing sugar in a bowl and mix well. Pipe filling into cannelloni with a piping bag.

Pour over raspberry sauce and serve.

Pant Mawr Baked Cheesecake

Serves 2–4

150g/6 oz Pant Mawr Goat's Cheese in Plain Olive Oil
75g/3 oz sugar
2 eggs
1 tsp lemon juice
1 tsp vanilla essence

Pre-heat oven 180°C/350F/Gas mark 4.

Lightly butter two 225ml ramekins.

Blend together the Pant Mawr Goat's Cheese, sugar, eggs, vanilla essence and lemon juice until smooth.

Divide the mixture between the two prepared ramekins and bake until the tops are golden brown, approximately 35–40 minutes.

Allow the cheesecake to cool, then chill completely before serving.

Serve with a dollop of cream and grated chocolate to garnish.

Apple Pie with Caerphilly Pastry

Serves 6

Pastry
350g/12 oz plain flour
pinch salt
100g/4 oz butter
50g/2 oz Caerphilly Cheese
cold water to bind

900g/2 lb ready-sliced apples, defrosted
demerara sugar

Combine the apple slices and sugar.

Sieve the flour into a bowl with the salt. Using your fingertips, gently rub the butter and Caerphilly Cheese into the flour, then add water a little at a time until the mixture forms a small ball of dough. Leave the pastry to rest and cover with cling film.

Roll out pastry on to an oven-proof plate. Sprinkle bottom layer with a little sugar. Place apple filling in the centre, then roll out the rest of the pastry and place over the top, sealing the edges with a little water. Pinch edges all the way round with thumb and forefinger.

Bake in the oven for about 45 minutes at 160°C/325°F/Gas mark 3.

Caernarfon Cheese Pudding

Serves 3–4

600ml/1 pint milk
30g/1 oz butter
115g/4 oz breadcrumbs
90g/3½ oz Old Shire Cheddar Cheese, grated
2 eggs, beaten

Heat milk and butter together until just boiling, and pour over breadcrumbs. Whisk to a smooth consistency, then add Old Shire Cheddar Cheese, season to taste, and stir in beaten eggs.

Transfer mixture to a buttered oven-proof dish and bake for 30–35 minutes at 180°C/ 350°F/Gas mark 4.

Welsh Cheddar
Savoury Cheese Muffins

Makes 16 Muffins

300g/10 oz flour
2 tbsp baking powder
1 tsp ground ginger
1 tsp ground pepper
2 eggs
1½ cups of milk
100g/4 oz melted butter
100g/4 oz Aeron Valley Cheddar, grated

Sift the flour with baking powder, ginger and pepper.

Mix together the eggs, milk and Aeron Valley Cheddar. Make a well in the centre of the bowl and pour in the egg and cheese mixture. Stir gently with a holed spoon until the batter is just mixed then fold through the butter. Lift the mixture up with the spoon, turning it over on top of the remaining mixture. Repeat the lifting until all ingredients are all just blended.

Three quarter fill 16 well-greased muffin tins.

Bake at 220°C/425°F/Gas mark 7 for 15–20 minutes until well-risen and golden.

Poppy Seed Cheese Loaf

3 tbsp poppy seeds
450g/1 lb plain flour
2 tbsp baking powder
1½ tsp salt
1 tsp baking soda
175g/6 oz Aeron Valley Cheddar, grated
3 onions, finely chopped
4 eggs
450ml/16 fl oz buttermilk

Soak poppy seeds in hot water for about 10 minutes, then drain and dry well on kitchen paper. In a large bowl, combine the flour, baking powder, salt and baking soda. Stir in the seeds, Aeron Valley Cheddar, and onion. Make a well in the centre, add the eggs, and whisk together until frothy. Whisk in the buttermilk and quickly mix in the flour. The mixture should be lumpy.

Grease 3 small loaf tins well.

Divide the mix between the 3 loaf tins and bake for about 35 minutes or until a knife inserted into the centre of the loaf comes out clean.

Already published
in the _It's Wales_ series:

More to follow!